MINERALS

by

Roy A. Gallant

BENCHMARK BOOKS

MARSHALL CAVENDISH
NEW YORK

Series consultant:
Christopher J. Schuberth
Division of Curriculum & Instruction
Armstrong State College

Benchmark Books
99 White Plains Road
Tarrytown, New York 10591-9001

Library of Congress Cataloging-in-Publication Data
Gallant, Roy A.
Minerals / by Roy A. Gallant
        p. cm. — (Kaleidoscope)
Includes bibliographical references and index.
Summary: Describes the composition of minerals, their physical properties, and how they are formed.
ISBN 0-7614-1039-2
1. Minerals—Juvenile literature. [1. Minerals.] I. Title. II. Kaleidoscope (Tarrytown, N.Y.)
QE365.2 .G35 2001   549—dc21   99-046100

Photo research by Candlepants Incorporated
Cover photo: Photo Researchers/Charles D. Winters
The photographs in this book are used by permission and through the courtesy of:
Photo Researchers: Andrew Syred/Science Photo Library, 5; /Michael Kuh, 9; /E. R. Degginger, 10; Mahau Kulyk/Science Photo Library, 13; Dr. Jeremy Burgess/Science Photo Library, 18, 25; /Gary Retherford, 26; /Charles D. Winters, 29, 30, 42; /V. B. Scheffer, 33; /Douglas Faulkner, 34; /Lowell Georgia, 41. CORBIS: Jeff Vanuga, 6; Ron Watts, 14; Adam Woolfitt, 17; Kevin R. Morris, 22; Jeremy Horner, 37; Jim Sugar Photography, 38.

Printed in Italy

6 5 4 3 2 1

CONTENTS

WHAT ARE MINERALS?

Have you ever tasted a mineral? Of course you have. Salt is a mineral. You even write with a mineral. The "lead" in a pencil is actually the mineral graphite. Minerals are everywhere. They are even inside your computer. There is copper in its wires and silicon in its memory chips. Both copper and silicon come from minerals.

Tiny flakes of graphite, not "lead," are the marks a pencil leaves behind.

6

Did you know that you can grow mineral crystals in a beautiful mineral garden? After you finish reading about minerals, you will find out how to "plant" your own mineral garden and watch it grow. But first, let's find out what minerals are and what they look and feel like.

Most minerals are made deep inside Earth. Others are made at or near its surface. Either way, they are the building blocks of rocks. So when you pick up a rock, you're really holding a clump of minerals.

Sculpted by the wind, this stone arch is also a loop full of minerals.

Some minerals are solid *elements*, such as gold, silver, and diamond. Others are *compounds*, meaning two or more elements combined. The salt you use at the dinner table is a compound. It is made of the two elements sodium and chlorine. In total, there are about four thousand minerals. Most of them are compounds.

When you take the water out of ocean water, what do you have left? White piles of sea salt.

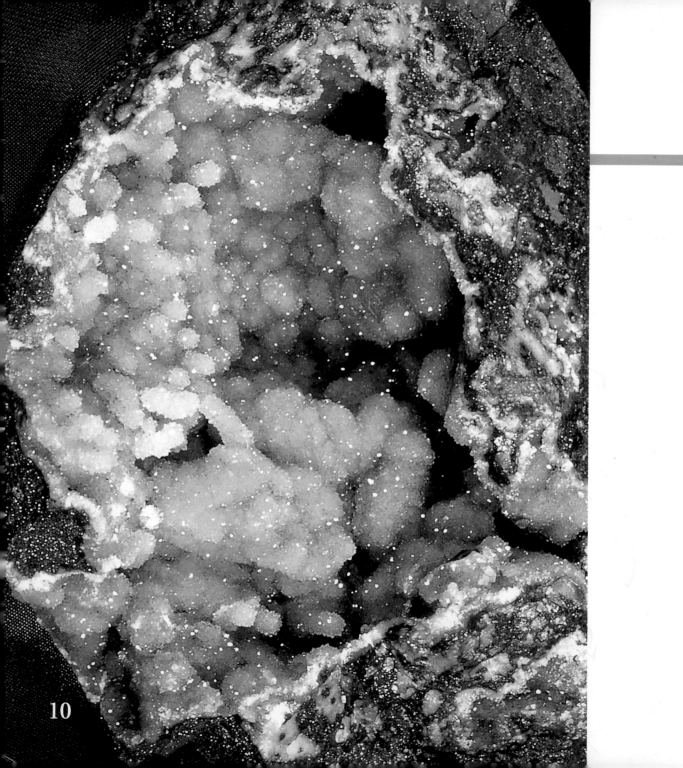

10

BUILDING BLOCKS

Rocks are made of minerals. But what makes up a mineral? The answer is crystals. The next time you're at the beach, pick up a handful of sand. As the sand sifts through your fingers, notice how some of the grains sparkle in the light. These are tiny pieces of the mineral quartz. The small grains are *crystalline*. That means they are solid substances with flat surfaces and a shape they all have in common. Coins, spaceships, and the metal in bridges are made up of crystalline substances.

Clumps of quartz cover this mineral, chrysocolla, from Australia.

Snowflakes, icicles, and mountains are made up of crystals as well. The next time you come across a freshly broken rock, look at it with a magnifying glass. You'll be able to see the tiny, gleaming crystals of many different minerals.

Snowflakes are beautiful six-sided crystals when they form slowly in calm air. If a flake is cut down the middle, the two halves match perfectly.

13

Mineral crystals form regular patterns. The crystal pattern of a mineral such as gold, for example, is repeated over and over all the way through the piece of gold. Likewise, the crystal patterns of diamond and silver are always the same, whether these minerals were dug up in Russia, in India, or in your backyard.

A crystal? No. But crystals have repeating patterns of atoms just like the repeating blocks of windows in a skyscraper.

Of all the different kinds of minerals found in nature, no two have the same crystal pattern. Like a fingerprint, each mineral has its own crystal pattern. Just as detectives can identify criminals by their fingerprints, geologists can identify minerals by looking at their crystal patterns.

Like a detective looking through a magnifying glass, this man is making sure the diamond is real.

18

CRYSTAL CLUES

Drop a pinch of salt on a flat surface, and then look at the grains with a magnifying glass or a low-power microscope. Each grain is a crystal in the shape of a cube. Some may have been nicked by bumping against each other. But you should be able to find many nearly perfect cubes. They will all look exactly alike. Crush a salt grain with a spoon. What appears to be powder is a group of tinier cubes, just like the larger cubes you can see.

A salt grain as seen by a high-power microscope. The cubes are all alike, except where the edges have been nicked or broken off.

Many mineral crystals have more complex shapes than salt. Some are long triangular needles. Others, such as asbestos, come in a mass of threads. Crystals can be grouped by their shapes. Look at the diagram. Zircon is the shape of two small pyramids stuck together at the base. Geologists can measure the crystal faces to figure out what kind of mineral they have.

The crystals of each mineral have their own special shape. Here is a view of six.

COMMON CRYSTAL SHAPES

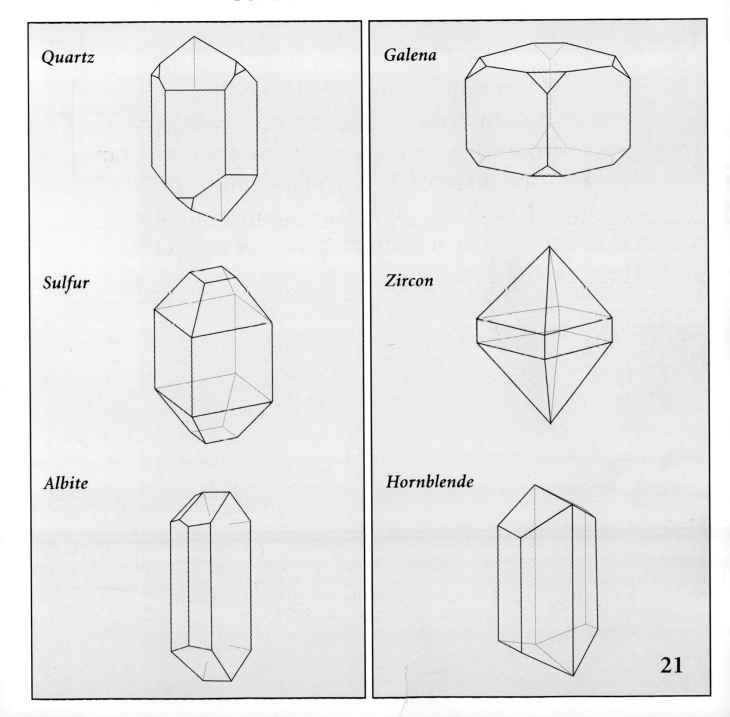

Quartz

Galena

Sulfur

Zircon

Albite

Hornblende

FAMILY RESEMBLANCE

Did you know that an ounce of gold can be hammered thin enough to cover an entire football field? That is an example of one of the *physical properties* of gold. Each mineral has its own set of physical properties. These properties can help you tell one mineral from another.

Gold can be hammered into many shapes. This Buddhist stupa, or shrine, in Myanmar has been covered in the prized metal.

Here are some common mineral properties:

Hardness

Some minerals are hard, while others are soft. A mineral's hardness is based on how easily it can be scratched by another mineral. A harder mineral will always scratch a softer one. One of the softest minerals in nature is talc. Soapstone is talc. Sculptors like soapstone because it is easy to carve.

You can write with a pencil because its graphite crystals are held together so weakly that they slip apart, break free, and stick to the paper. Graphite is a form of the element carbon. So are diamonds. But diamond crystals form in a different way. They are very strong and do not break apart easily. Diamond is the hardest substance known in nature.

On a record player the stylus, or needle, is often made of diamond so it won't chip or break.

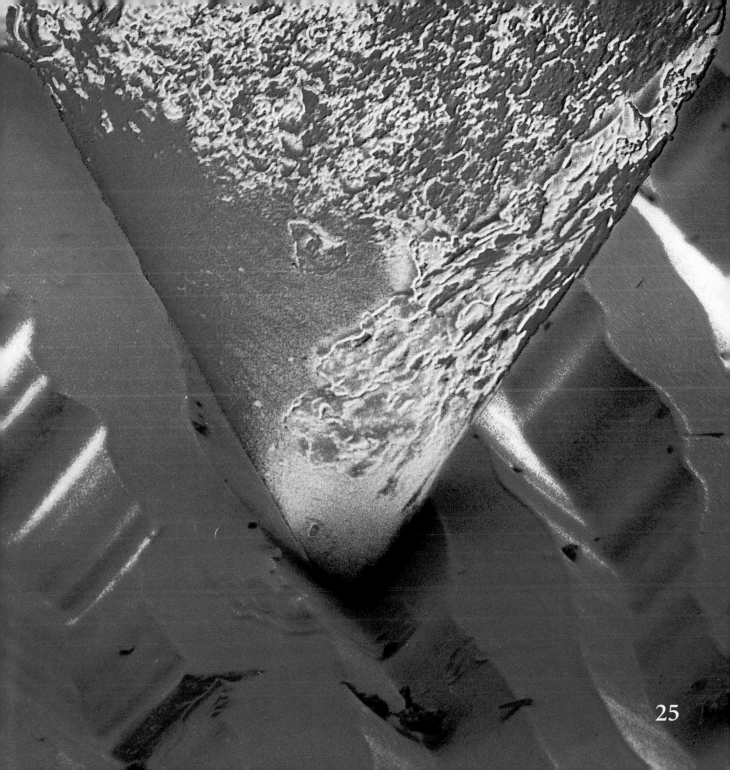

25

Color

Minerals come in an endless number of colors. Some are beautifully colored gemstones. The dazzling red of the mineral ruby has long made that gemstone a favorite. And there is the transparent blue of sapphire, the dark green of malachite, the deep blue of azurite, and the shiny bronze of copper.

Color is a mineral's easiest physical property to identify. But color can also be the most misleading. Only a few minerals are always the same color. Most come in different colors. The mineral quartz, for example, may be clear, milky, or rose colored.

Azurite takes its name from azure, a shade of blue.

Streak

When you scratch a mineral against a piece of unglazed tile, the mineral will leave a streak of powder. The color of the streak is a clue to the kind of mineral you have. For example, the mineral fluorite always leaves a white streak. That is true even though fluorite comes in different colors.

Luster

Luster is another word for shine. The way a mineral shines when you hold it under light helps you identify it. One mineral may glow with a bright metallic luster while another is dull. Among the words that describe a mineral's luster are pearly, waxy, greasy, glassy, and silky. Graphite, for example, has a metallic luster. Fluorite is glassy. Talc is silky.

Fluorite (lower right) is glassy. Calcite (lower left) is clear. In the back, iron pyrite gives off a metallic luster. Iron pyrite has tricked many fortune hunters, thus its nickname, fool's gold.

30

Heft

A mineral's *density*, or how much matter is packed into it, means how heavy it feels. For example, a piece of iron feels much heavier than a lump of coal of the same size.

Breakage

A mineral breaks apart in one of two ways. If it breaks with rough edges, like a pencil snapped in two, we call the break a *fracture*. But if it breaks by coming apart in flat sheets, we call the break *cleavage*. Mica cleaves nicely into flat, paper-thin sheets. But if you try to break one of the sheets in two, it will fracture.

This mineral breaks neatly into sheets that can be easily peeled away. The conclusion? It's mica.

Other Properties

Some minerals, such as magnetite, are attracted by a magnet, but most are not. Others glow in bright colors when held under an ultraviolet lamp. The glow is called *fluorescence*. Certain parts of the mineral calcite shine bright red. Willemite shines with an intense green. Fluorite, where the word fluorescence comes from, glows a strong blue.

Many minerals give off fluorescent light. If you shine ultraviolet light on franlinite, it has a pinkish glow.

33

Water erodes, or washes away, the land. Clay, soil, and other matter are swept into the ocean. Someday, these sediments will become rock.

FORGED BENEATH OUR FEET

Minerals are made up of *sediments*, small chunks of clay, mud, and sand. These sediments are washed off the land by rivers and streams. They are then carried far out onto the seafloor. Over millions of years, more and more sediments pile up. Their great weight presses the bottom sediments ever deeper into the seafloor. The heat and pressure become so great that the deep sediments are turned into solid rock. The kinds of mineral crystals that form in these rocks depend on the chemical makeup of the clay, mud, and sand.

The deep new rock in which mineral crystals have formed is heated so much that the rock becomes soft like putty. It can be squeezed this way and that, like toothpaste in a tube. The rock is pressed so hard that the shape of its mineral crystals can change. That means that one kind of mineral can turn into a different one. For millions of years, heat and pressure have been changing the planet's deeply buried rock and its minerals. Over time, that sunken rock may be thrust up as a new mountain range full of glistening minerals.

Millions of years in the making, colorful stripes of minerals tower over a village in Argentina.

37

Minerals can form another way. When pockets of melted rock called *magma* are forced up through cracks in Earth's crust, they pour out over the ground as lava. If the lava cools slowly, it has plenty of time to form large mineral grains. An example of such large grains are those found in a type of rock called granite. If the lava cools quickly, its atoms do not have time to arrange themselves into mineral crystals at all. Instead, volcanic glass, known as obsidian, is formed.

The eruption of a volcano is always an amazing sight. Time decides whether these rivers of lava will become mineral grains or obsidian.

MINERALS WE'VE KNOWN

Minerals serve us in countless ways. We wear sparkling diamonds, rubies, and emeralds. The little white "M" printed on M&M candies comes from two minerals called rutile and ilmenite. When combined and turned into a powder, these minerals turn paint and toothpaste white. They also are the white coating on powdered doughnuts and in the filling in an Oreo cookie.

Here, a miner holds a chunk of coal that will fuel a furnace or light a home.

Quartz crystals are used in our watches to keep accurate time. Tiny pieces of diamond and sapphire are the balls in expensive ballpoint pens. Diamonds are also used as drill tips. Those minerals, and all the others that we use each day, were forged miles beneath our feet in Earth's crust millions of years ago. New minerals are being made as you read these words, and older ones are being recycled in a process that never ends.

Minerals come in an endless variety—white, spiky gypsum (lower left), blue-green azurite (top), and metallic clumps of copper (lower right).

GROWING A CRYSTAL GARDEN

Many craft shops sell crystal-growing kits, but you can start your very own crystal farm with some simple items you'll find around the house or at the supermarket. You might need to ask an adult for help. Here is what you'll need to get started:

Food coloring
3 or 4 pieces of sponge about the size of a marshmallow
6 tablespoons of water
6 tablespoons of laundry blueing
6 tablespoons of salt
1 tablespoon of ammonia
A soup bowl

Mix the water, salt, and laundry blueing in a glass or jar. Then, add the ammonia. Place the sponge pieces in the soup bowl. Make sure there is room between each piece. Now pour the liquid over them.

Watch as little towers of crystals begin to grow on the sponge pieces. How high do the towers get after an hour? To color your crystal garden, carefully drip small amounts of food coloring onto the pieces of sponge. Every day, sprinkle a little more salt over your garden and add a few more teaspoons of water and laundry blueing. But be careful not to bump the soup bowl. Otherwise, the fragile towers will fall over.

GLOSSARY

cleavage   The way a mineral splits in one or more directions along smooth surfaces.

compound   Any substance made up of two or more elements combined.

crystalline   Any substance that is made of crystals.

density   The amount of matter packed into a given space.

element   Any substance that is made up of the same kinds of atoms repeated over and over. Gold, carbon, and oxygen are elements.

fluorescence   The glow given off by some minerals when an ultraviolet light is shined on them.

fracture   The jagged way in which some minerals break.

magma   Liquid rock coming from the deeper parts of Earth's crust. It flows out of volcanoes as lava.

physical property   A trait, such as hardness, color, and heft, that helps identify a mineral.

sediment   Sand, mud, and clay carried by a river and often washed out onto the seafloor.

FIND OUT MORE

Books:

Angliss, Sarah. *Gold.* Tarrytown, NY: Marshall Cavendish, 2000.

Blashfield, Jean F. *Sodium.* Chatham, NJ: Raintree Steck-Vaughn, 1999.

Bown, Deni. *Rocks and Minerals.* New York: DK Publishing, 1995.

Christian, Spenser, and Antonia Felix. *Is There a Dinosaur in Your Backyard? The World's Most Fascinating Fossils, Rocks, and Minerals.* New York: John Wiley & Sons, 1998.

Curtis, Neil. *Rocks and Minerals.* New York: Oxford University Press, 1998.

Dixon, Dougal. *Rocks and Minerals.* New York: Penguin, 1997.

Krause, Barry. *Mineral Collector's Handbook.* New York: Sterling, 1996.

Lye, Keith. Rocks, *Minerals and Fossils.* Parsippany, NJ: Silver Burdett, 1991.

Packard, Mary. *Rocks and Minerals.* Mahwah, NJ: Troll, 1997.

Parker, Steve. *Rocks and Minerals.* New York: DK Publishing, 1993.

Pinet, Michele. *Be Your Own Rock and Mineral Expert.* New York: Sterling, 1997.

Quinn, Greg H. *Minerals.* New York: Scholastic, 1995.

Ricciuti, Edward R. *National Audubon Society First Field Guide: Rocks and Minerals.* New York: Scholastic, 1998.

Russell, William. *Rocks and Minerals.* Vero Beach, FL: Rourke, 1994.

Websites:

Mineral Gallery
www.theimage.com/mineral/minerals1.html

Smithsonian Gem and Mineral Collection
galaxy.einet.net/images/gems/gems%2Dicons.html

Rocks and Minerals for Kids
tqjunior.advanced.org/3639/

Hiroyasu's Private Mineral Museum
village.infoweb.or.jp/%7Efwge0853/indcx.htm

Agates from the Land of Pumas and Craters
www.rockhounds.com/rockgem/articles/agates.html

Crystal Caves
www.crystalcaves.com.au/page3.html

Oklahoma Crystal Collecting
www.oklahoma.cc/

AUTHOR'S BIO

Roy A. Gallant, called "one of the deans of American science writers for children" by *School Library Journal,* is the author of more than eighty books on scientific subjects. Since 1979, he has been director of the Southworth Planetarium at the University of Southern Maine, where he holds an adjunct full professorship. He lives in Rangeley, Maine.

INDEX

Page numbers for illustrations are in boldface.